FISH

Troll Associates

FISH

by Louis Sabin

Illustrated by Jean Helmer

Troll Associates

Library of Congress Cataloging in Publication Data

Sabin, Louis.
  Fish.

  Summary: Describes many kinds of fish, from the tiny
pygmy goby to the gigantic whale shark, and explains
how they live.
  1. Fishes—Juvenile literature. [1. Fishes]
I. Helmer, Jean Cassels, ill. II. Title.
QL617.2.S23   1984   597   84-2624
ISBN 0-8167-0178-4 (lib. bdg.)
ISBN 0-8167-0179-2 (pbk.)

Most of the Earth is covered by water—
ponds, swamps, lakes, rivers, streams, and
oceans. And in just about all of them there
are fish. There are more than twenty
thousand species of fish in the world.

The smallest fish is the pygmy goby, which is the size of the nail on your big toe. The largest fish is the whale shark, which can grow to be as long as a railroad car. There are long, thin fish and fat, round fish. Some are brightly colored, and others are muddy brown and gray. But no matter what their size, how they look, and where they live, all fish have three things in common.

First, fish have a skeleton with a backbone. Shellfish, such as lobsters, crabs, and clams, are not fish, because they have outside shells instead of internal backbones.

Second, all fish have gills that let them breathe in the water. Whales and dolphins are not fish, because they have lungs instead of gills.

And third, all fish are cold-blooded. This means their body temperature is about the same as the temperature of the water they swim in.

Most fish live in the water all the time. But a few, like the mudskipper, spend a part of their time out of the water. All fish breathe with the aid of gills. But a few, like the lungfish, also use lungs to take in air. And most fish have scaly skins. But some, like certain eels and the sea horse, have no scales.

Fish are divided into three classes—the jawless fish, the cartilaginous fish, and the bony fish. The jawless fish, such as the hagfish and lamprey, are parasites. They use their round, sucking mouths to attach themselves to other fish and to take their food from their unwilling hosts.

Sharks and rays are cartilaginous fish. That means their backbones are made of cartilage instead of bone. Cartilage is a flexible tissue that is not as hard as bone. Your nose and ears are made of cartilage.

The largest and best-known class of fish contains the bony fish. These include trout, salmon, flounder, the powerful tarpon, and the popular goldfish.

There is one kind of bony fish, the coelacanth, that was thought to be extinct for millions of years. Then scientists discovered living coelacanths in the waters off the coast of Africa. This was an especially exciting discovery because an ancient relative of the coelacanth is thought to be the ancestor of all reptiles, amphibians, birds, and mammals.

No matter how different fish may look on the outside, most of them are very similar on the inside. They have a skeleton made up of a skull, a backbone that runs from the base of the skull to the tail, and fin supports. Fin supports are small bones that give shape to the dorsal fin, which is located on the fish's back. Fish use the dorsal fin to keep from rolling over as they swim.

There is another fin, at the bottom of a fish's body, that works along with the dorsal fin to maintain the fish's balance. There are also pectoral fins, behind the gills, and pelvic fins, which are like a pair of flippers, and the caudal fin, which is really the fish's tail.

All of these fins help the fish to change direction as they swim, and to slow or stop. Most fish swim by swinging their tails to one side while they curve their bodies to the other side. They move smoothly because their bodies are sleek and streamlined.

As a fish moves about, it takes in water through its mouth. This water flows past the gills on each side of the head and out beneath the gill covers. There are four gills on each side of the head of most fish. They are featherlike structures and usually red. The redness comes from the oxygen the fish breathes.

Gills work the way our lungs do. A fish's blood flows through the gills, where oxygen

is picked up and carbon-dioxide wastes are given off. Then the heart pumps the oxygen-rich blood through the arteries and into every part of the body.

Most fish have an air bladder, or "swim bladder," in the center of the body. The main use of the air bladder, which is like a long balloon, is to keep the fish from rising or sinking in the water. In some fish, it also acts as a storage tank for air.

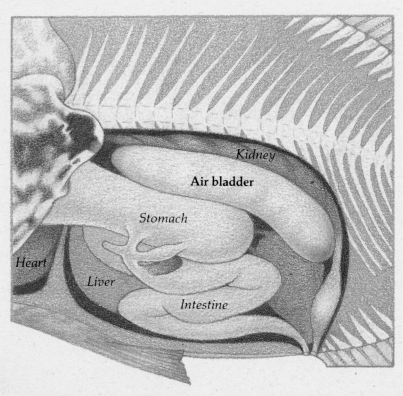

Because fish live underwater, they must also find their food underwater. Some fish eat only animals, such as insects, worms, shellfish, and other fish. Some eat only plants, such as seaweed. And some eat both plants and animals. Each species of fish has teeth suited to the food it eats.

Sharks have several rows of razor-sharp teeth, so if one tooth breaks off, another can move up to take its place. The pike has sharp, pointed teeth in its mouth and upper throat. These teeth are angled toward the back of the mouth to keep the fish caught by the pike from escaping.

Herring eat tiny plants and animals called plankton, which they strain out of the water with comblike "gill-rakers." They also have teeth, but the teeth are small and weak.

Fish that feed along the bottom generally have the mouth on the lower side of the head. And some, like the catfish, have whiskerlike feelers called barbels. These help the catfish to find food.

The flounder and the fluke, both of which spend most of their time lying on the ocean floor, have both eyes on the same side of their heads. The hammerhead shark is shaped like the capital letter "T," with the head as the crossbar. This shark's eyes are at the ends of the crossbar, and it can see a large part of the sea around it. Some fish that live their whole lives in the deepest parts of the ocean or in underwater caves are blind. They find their food by touch and smell.

All fish can smell, but in some kinds of fish, the sense of smell is particularly well developed. One example is Atlantic salmon, which are born in freshwater streams. Then they travel many miles to the sea, where they live for years, until they are ready to lay eggs. Then they travel back to the streams where they were born. The salmon do this by following the smells they remember from their journey downstream.

Fish also "hear sounds," even though they have no outside ears. They feel sound vibrations that travel through the water.

Fish also have a sense organ that runs along their sides from front to back. It is called the lateral-line system. Inside the lateral line are clusters of sense organs that pick up movement, vibrations, and the slightest change in the flow of water. The lateral line helps a fish to find food, stay with its school, and escape its enemies.

Different fish protect themselves from enemies by doing different things. The porcupine fish has long, sharp spines that stick out from the body when the fish is frightened. The swordfish uses speed to

escape its enemies. The scorpion fish has sharp spines that are poisonous. Electric eels produce a strong electrical shock. And many fish hide from enemies by blending with their background.

Every fish, no matter how large or small, was once in an egg. In a few species, including the sharks, the male and female mate, and the eggs hatch inside the female's body. Then the young fish are born alive. But most fish spawn, or lay their eggs in the water, where they are then fertilized by the male.

Most fish do not protect their eggs at all. Instead, they lay huge numbers of eggs at a time. This way, at least a few will survive the dangers that surround them. But some species watch over their eggs or protect them in some way. The firemouth cichlids, for example, carry their eggs in their mouths. After the eggs hatch, the young stay with their parents, swimming back into their mouths to escape enemies.

Some species of fish, including the salmon, migrate to a place where their eggs will be safe, then cover them with gravel, to protect them from discovery.

Eels, whether they live in North America or in Europe, migrate thousands of miles to

lay their eggs. Their destination is the Sargasso Sea, an area of the Atlantic Ocean near Bermuda. After they lay their eggs, the adult eels die. When the eggs hatch, the young eels instinctively migrate to the places from which their parents came.

Fish also migrate because they are cold-blooded—they cannot keep their body temperature constant. So if the water turns very cold, the fish's blood gets very cold. If it moves into warmer waters, its blood gets warmer. Water that is too cold or too hot will kill a fish.

And so, to stay alive, fish are almost always on the move—gliding swiftly and gracefully through their watery world.